D0713021

Woodpeckers

ABDO
Publishing Company
A Buddy Book
by
Julie Murray

VISIT US AT
www.abdopub.com

Published by Buddy Books, an imprint of ABDO Publishing Company, 4940 Viking Drive, Suite 622, Edina, Minnesota 55435. Copyright © 2005 by Abdo Consulting Group, Inc. International copyrights reserved in all countries. No part of this book may be reproduced in any form without written permission from the publisher.

Printed in the United States.

Edited by: Christy DeVillier
Contributing Editors: Matt Ray, Michael P. Goecke
Graphic Design: Maria Hosley
Image Research: Deborah Coldiron
Photographs: Corbis, Corel, Minden Pictures

Library of Congress Cataloging-in-Publication Data

Murray, Julie, 1969-
    Woodpeckers/Julie Murray.
        p. cm. — (Animal kingdom. Set II)
    Includes bibliographical references (p.).
    Contents: Birds — Woodpeckers — Size and color — Hammering — What they eat — Where they live — Their nests — Babies — The good and the bad.
    ISBN 1-59197-340-6
        1. Woodpeckers—Juvenile literature. [1. Woodpeckers.] I. Title.

QL696.P56M87 2003
598.7'2—dc21
                                                              2003044312

Contents

Woodpeckers

There are more than 9,000 kinds of birds. They live all around the world. All birds have wings and feathers. They have beaks and no teeth.

Birds live in many places around the world.

There are more than 200 kinds of woodpeckers. Woodpeckers are famous for hammering trees. This hammering makes a drumming sound. This sound tells people that woodpeckers are near.

Many people know the woodpecker's drumming sound.

What They Look Like

The pileated woodpecker is one of the largest woodpeckers in North America. It grows to become about 18 inches (46 cm) long.

A pileated woodpecker

One of the smallest woodpeckers is the Sunda woodpecker. Adults are about six inches (15 cm) long.

Most woodpeckers are black and white or brown and white. Males may have red or yellow feathers on their head.

Woodpeckers have strong feet for climbing trees.

Woodpeckers have a strong neck and beak for hammering wood. Stiff tail feathers help them **perch** in trees. Woodpeckers have strong, clawed feet for climbing, too.

Some male woodpeckers have red feathers on their head.

Where They Live

Woodpeckers live in North America, South America, Europe, Africa, and Asia. They can live in different **habitats**. Woodpeckers can live in hot places or cold places. The Gila woodpecker lives in the desert. Woodpeckers live in forests, mountains, and backyards, too. Most woodpeckers stay in one place their whole life.

Gila woodpeckers can
live in the dry desert.

Eating

Many woodpeckers look for food in trees. They hammer into tree bark to find insects and **larvae**. Woodpeckers catch insects with their long, sticky tongues. They eat ants, crickets, grasshoppers, and flies.

A woodpecker has been hammering at this tree.

Flicker woodpeckers often eat insects from the ground. Acorn woodpeckers eat acorns and store them inside trees. Sapsucker woodpeckers hammer at trees for **tree sap**. Woodpeckers also eat spiders, berries, nuts, and fruit.

This acorn woodpecker has many nuts stored in this tree.

Backyard Woodpeckers

Some people enjoy having woodpeckers in their backyard. They feed them birdseed and suet. Suet is animal fat. People can hang the suet in a tree. Backyard woodpeckers will eat suet all year long.

Suet mixed with birdseed is a treat for backyard woodpeckers.

Nests

In the spring, woodpeckers find mates. The male and the female build a nest together. Woodpeckers hammer large holes for their nests. Nests may be as deep as 18 inches (46 cm).

This Gila woodpecker has made a nest in a cactus.

Woodpeckers make nests in trees, telephone poles, and buildings. Most make a new nest every year. Other birds will use old woodpecker nests as their own.

A Campo flicker
and its nest.

Woodpecker Chicks

Female woodpeckers can lay as many as 10 eggs at one time. The eggs are white. The male and female woodpeckers take turns sitting on the eggs. They are keeping the eggs warm. This is called **incubation**.

The eggs hatch after two or three weeks. The newly hatched chicks are blind and featherless. The woodpecker parents bring them food.

Woodpeckers bring food to their chicks.

Chicks leave the nest
after about four weeks.

The chicks grow quickly. After about four weeks, they can live on their own. Some woodpeckers live as long as 10 years.

Important Words

habitat where an animal lives in the wild.

incubation keeping eggs warm before they hatch.

larvae young insects.

perch to rest in one place. Birds commonly perch on tree branches.

tree sap the sticky liquid inside trees.

Web Sites

To learn more about woodpeckers, visit ABDO Publishing Company on the World Wide Web. Web sites about woodpeckers are featured on our Book Links page. These links are routinely monitored and updated to provide the most current information available.

www.abdopub.com

Index